AF598884

She's Everything

Who is she?

She's infinite.

She's completely original;

she's impossible to define.

The easiest way to describe her is to say...

she's everything.

She's *fierce* about the things she loves—

the things that matter greatly.

But she meets the world with *gentleness*,

and tends to it carefully.

She's *fire and water* at the very same time.

She's the steadiest earth and the *wildest wind.*

She's *always growing.*

And always evolving...

again

and again

and again.

She's profound and she is *light.*

She is constant; she is *changing*.

And while she is always herself,

she is never

exactly the same.

She is often *courageous*.

And sometimes *afraid*.

She's an expert at continuing.

She meets the challenges anyway.

She's extraordinary,

even on the ordinary days.

She is deeply in her *head*,

and deeply in her *heart*.

She feels when she thinks,

and she thinks when she feels.

She is hugely,
impeccably,
beautifully real.

She knows what
to commit to.

And she knows how
to keep herself free.

She is so many things

without losing her authenticity.

She's *perfect* in her knowing that

she doesn't need to be.

There's fire in her heart,
so there is light in her eyes.

It touches everything around her, all the time.

She is not a single star,

but the *whole night sky.*

She's everything,

without trying.

She is *stronger* than anyone knows.

And she's tenderer, too.

Whatever she is doing,

her spirit shines through.

She is playful

and she's *wise*.

She stays true to herself.

This way, she can be true to everyone else.

She moves as the world moves. She *gives*

and she *takes*.

She shifts but she does not lose herself.

And her center does not break.

She makes an art of the *little things.*

And she makes the *big things* look easy.

She changes everything she touches.

and everyone she meets.

She makes things better, wherever she is.

Partly because she wants to. But partly,

it's just effortless.

She dreams *big dreams.*

And then, she makes them happen.

She shapes her world into being.

She's as vast and deep and

limitless as the sea.

She's more than she's ever been and yet,

not all that she will be.

There's a whole entire universe in everything she is.

And she is still becoming.

She's everything.

because she knows no other way of being.

Written by: M.H. Clark
Designed and Illustrated by: Justine Edge
Edited by: Bailey Vega

Library of Congress Control Number: 2022944075 | ISBN: 978-1957891-00-2

1st printing. Printed in China with soy inks on FSC®-Mix certified paper.